The First Exposure.

Curated by Kenneth Wong.
(@wasting.films on Instagram)

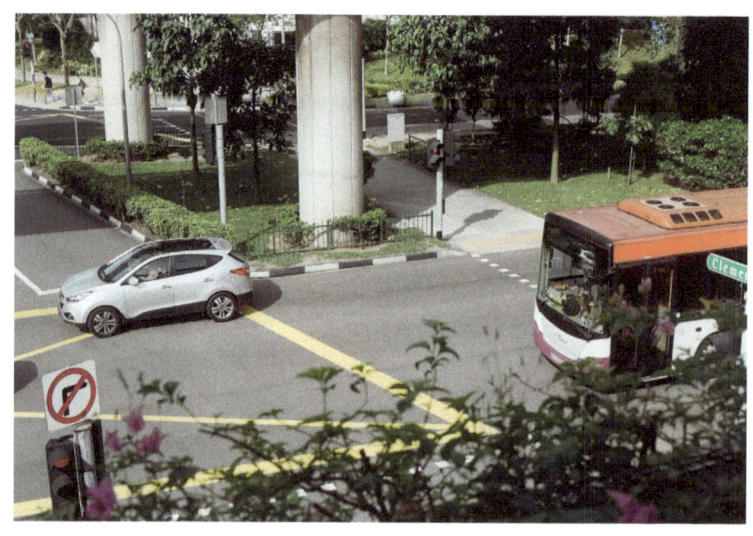

Canon AE-1 Program + Kodak Gold 200

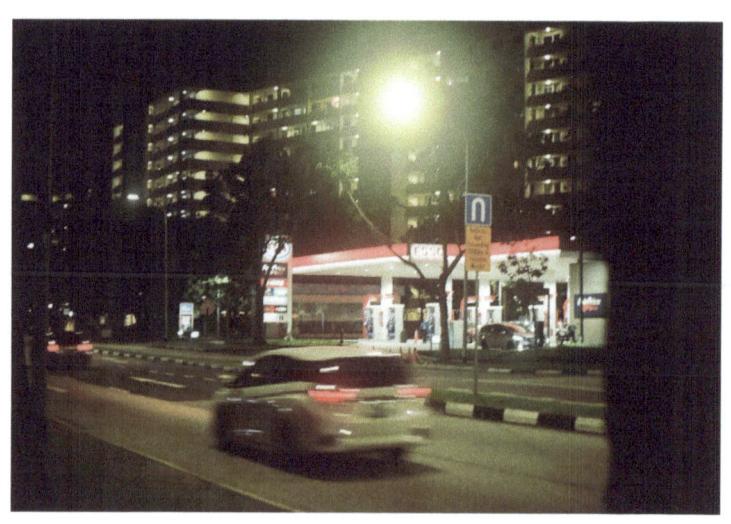

Canon AE-1 Program + Kodak Gold 200

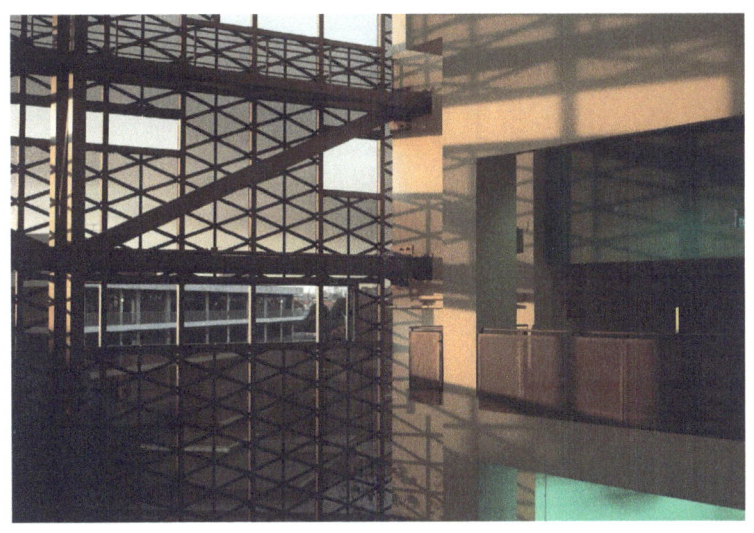

Canon AE-1 Program + Kodak Ultramax 400

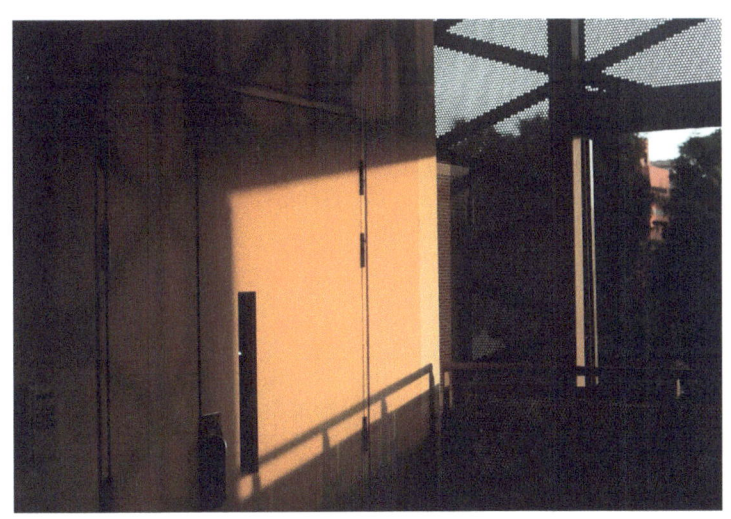

Canon AE-1 Program + Kodak Ultramax 400

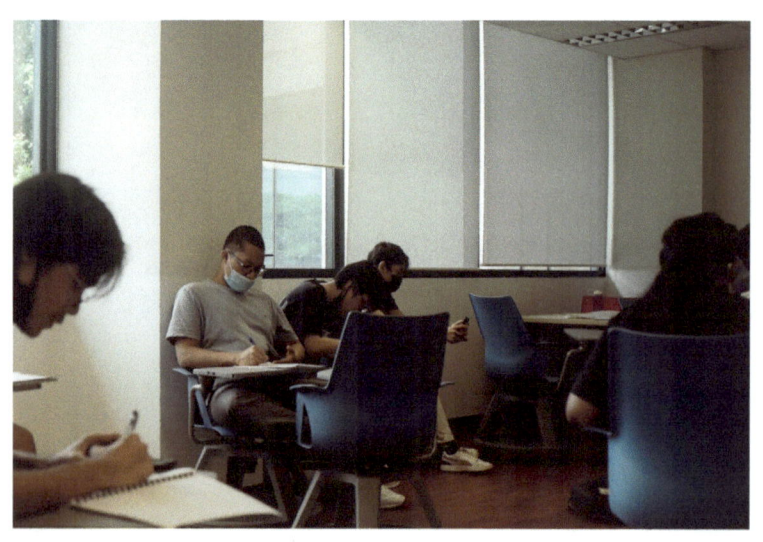

Canon AE-1 Program + Kodak Colorplus 200

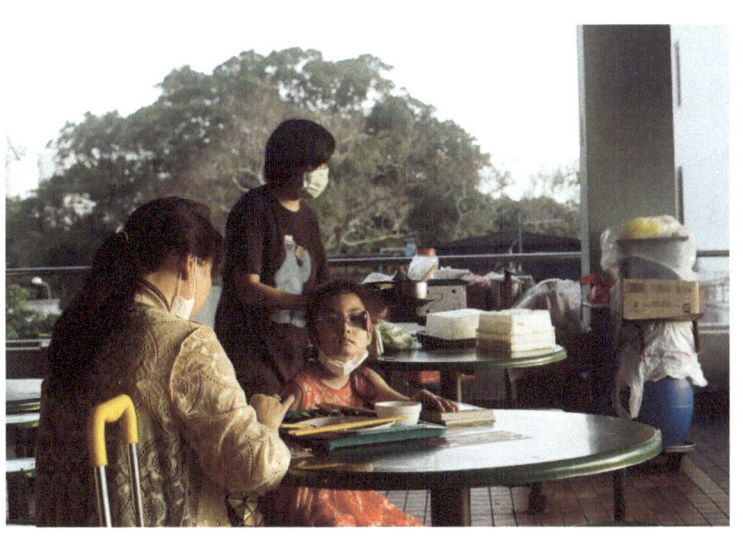

Canon AE-1 Program + Kodak Gold 200

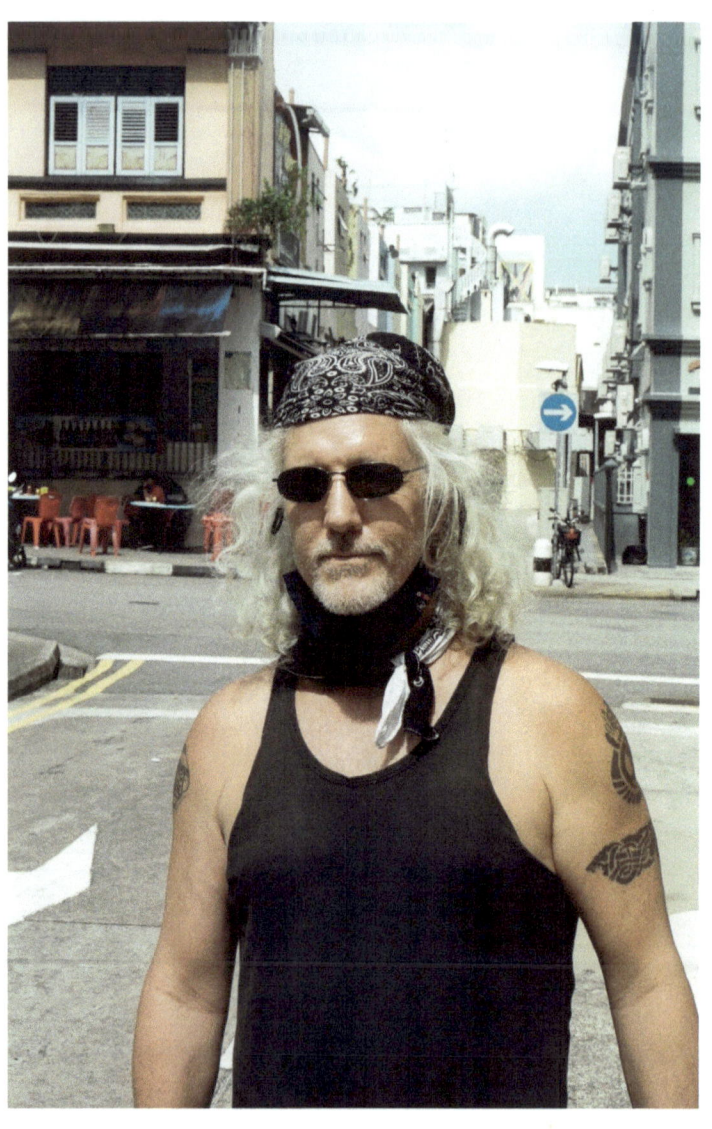

Dr D. Kyle Latinis//Canon AE-1 Program + Kodak Portra 400

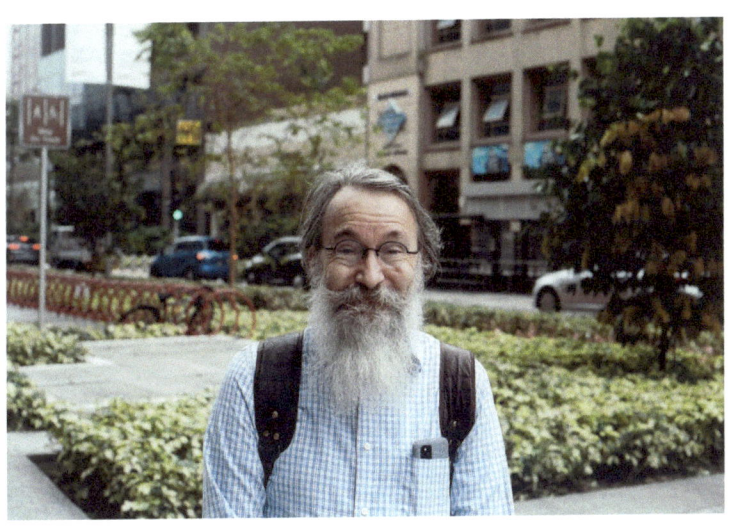

Canon AE-1 Program + Kodak Portra 400

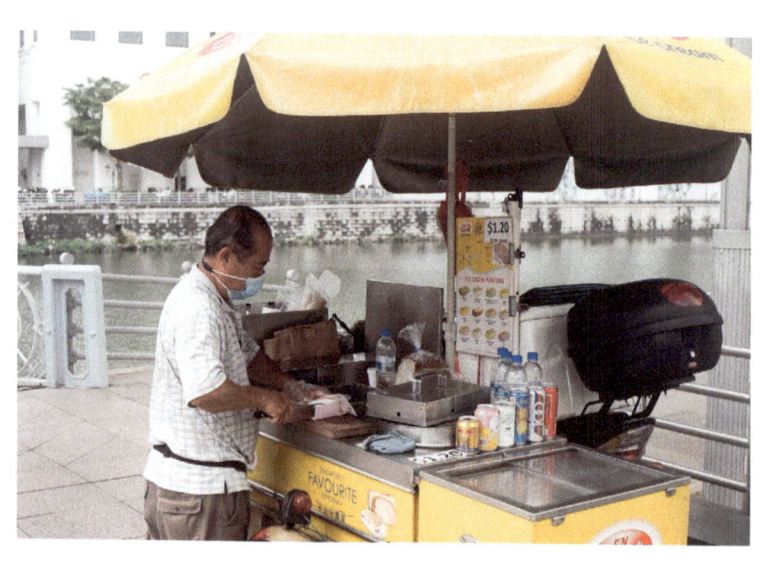

Canon AE-1 Program + Fuji Superia X-tra 400

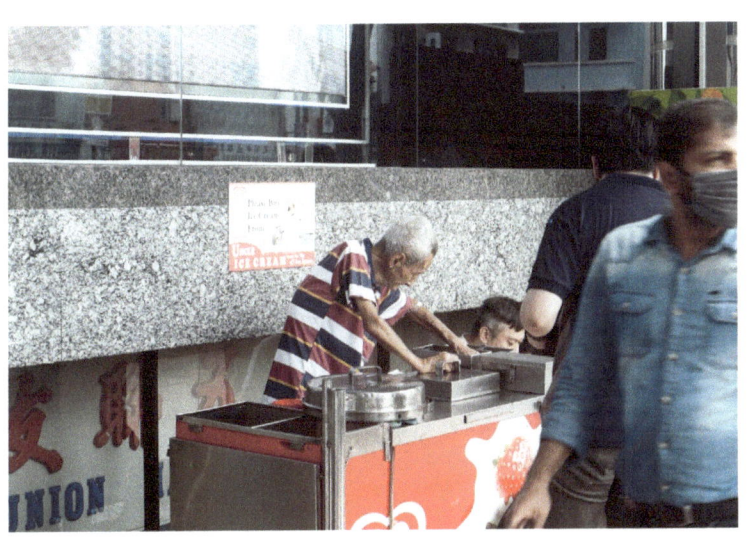

Canon AE-1 Program + Kodak Colorplus 200

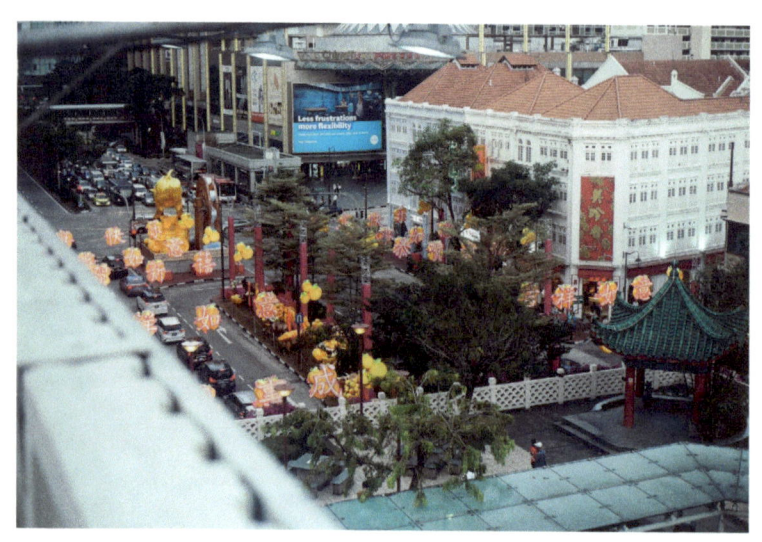

Canon AE-1 Program + Kodak Ultramax 400

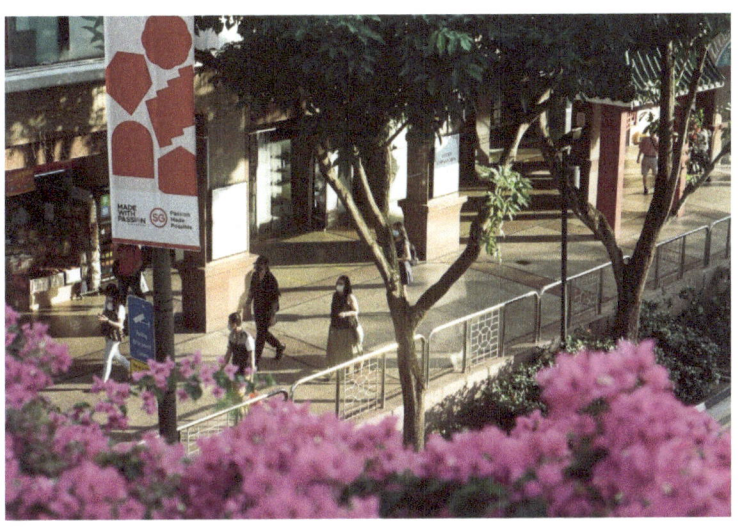

Canon AE-1 Program + Kodak Colorplus 200

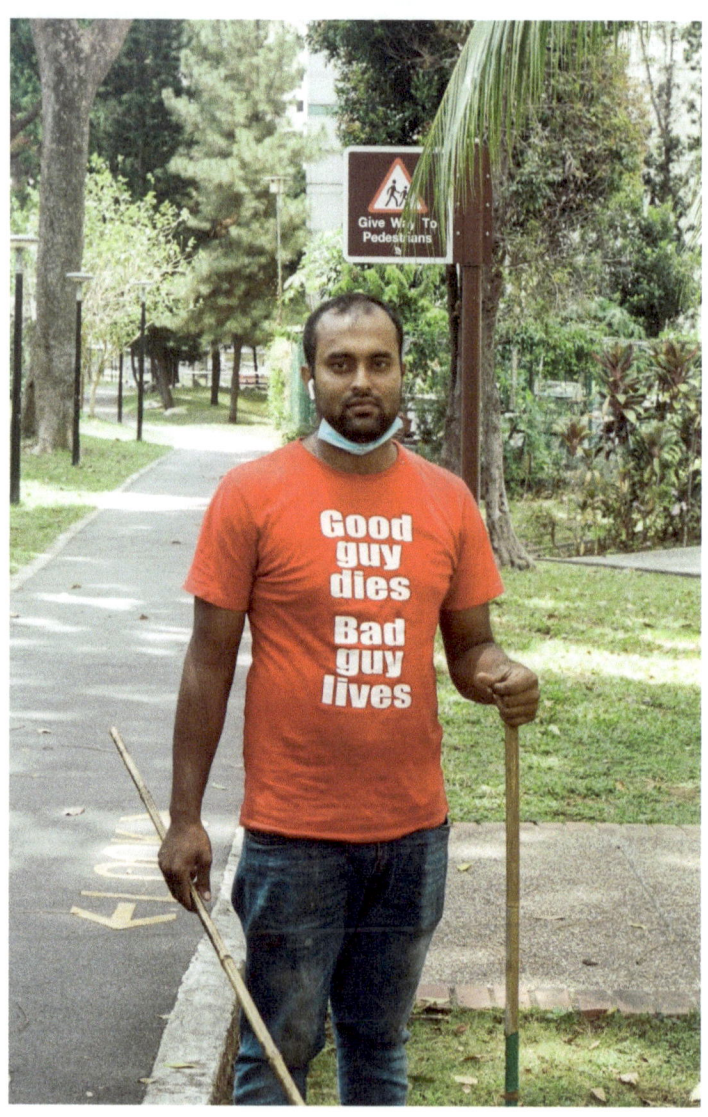

Canon AE-1 Program + Kodak Portra 400

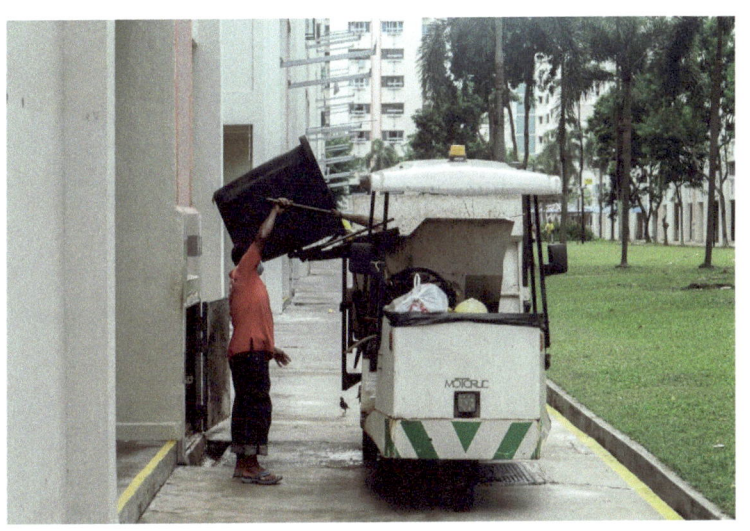

Canon AE-1 Program + Kodak Gold 200

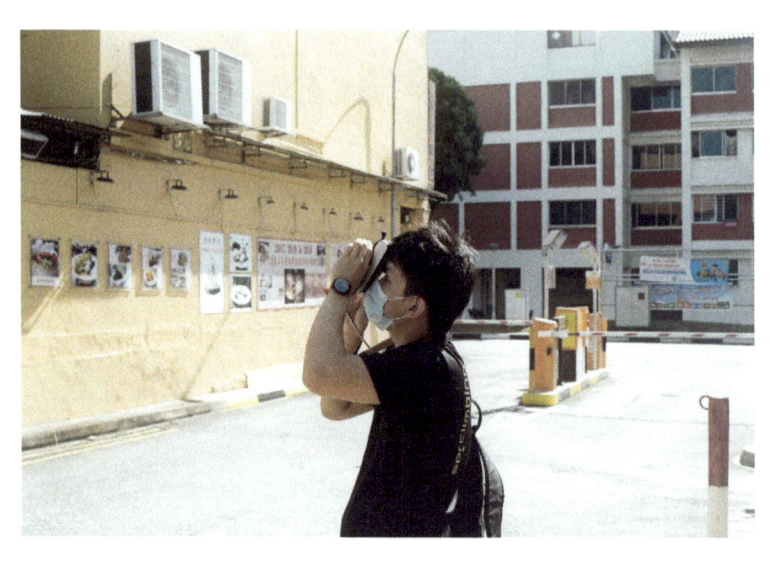

Canon AE-1 Program + Kodak Colorplus 200

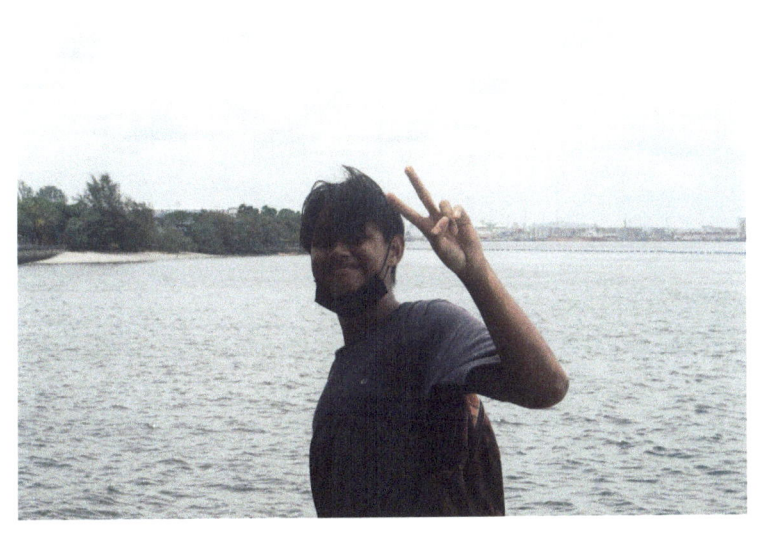

Canon AE-1 Program + Kodak Gold 200

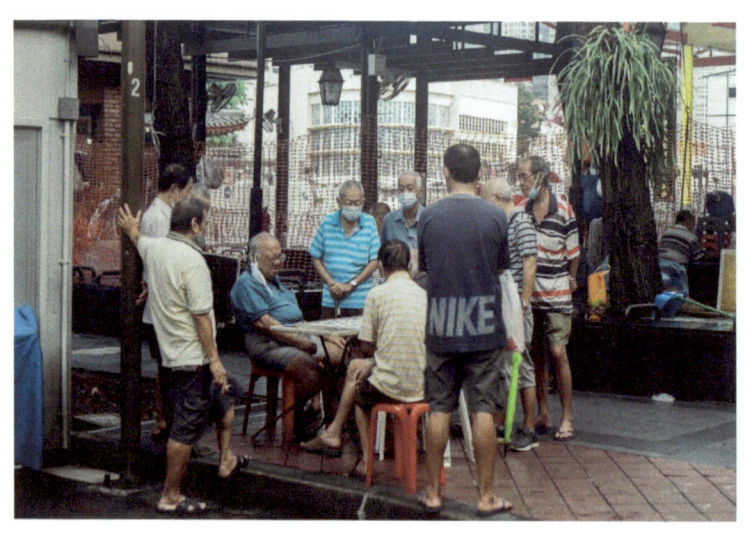

Canon AE-1 Program + Kodak ProImage 100

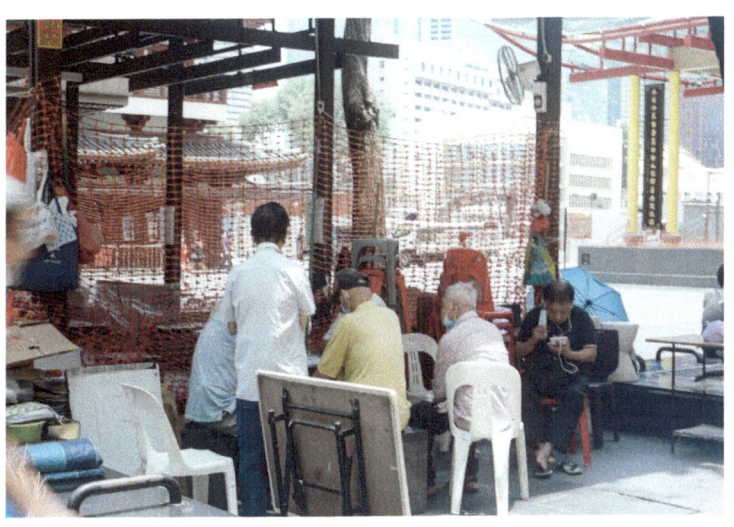

Canon AE-1 Program + Kodak Portra 400

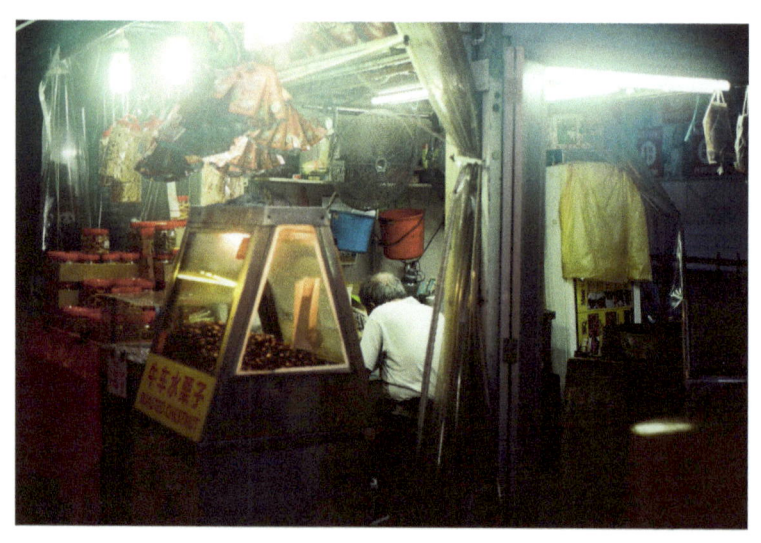

Canon AE-1 Program + Kodak Ultramax 400

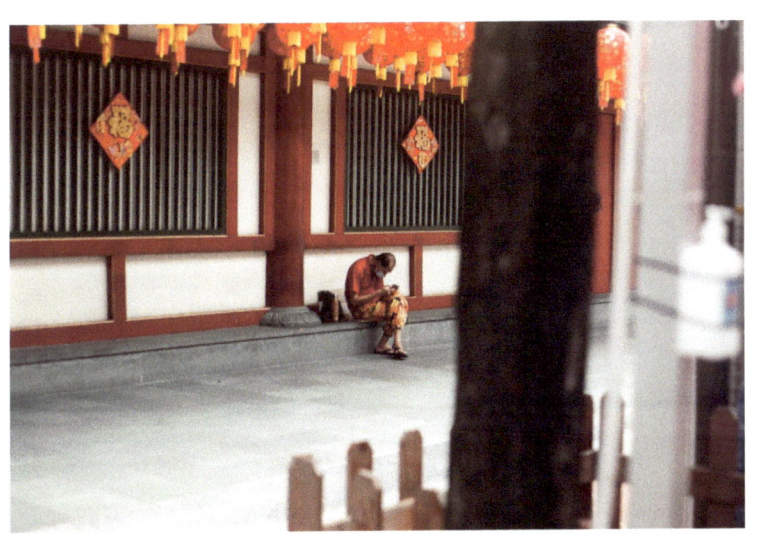

Canon AE-1 Program + Fuji Superia X-tra 400

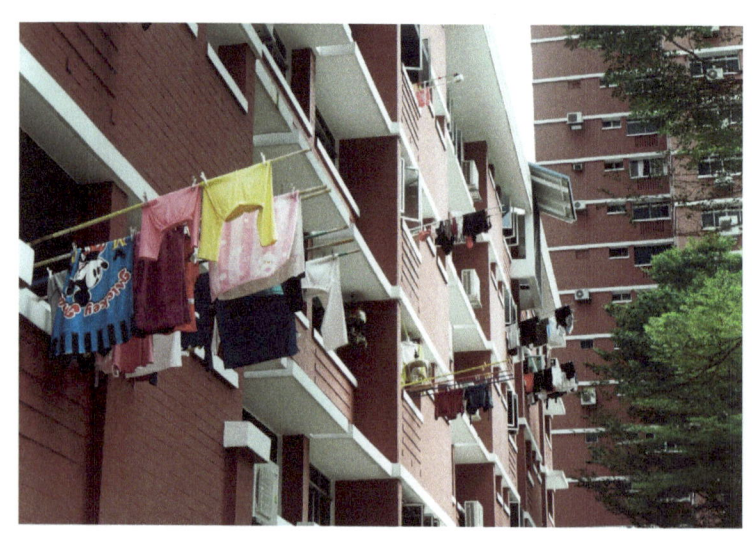

Canon AE-1 Program + Kodak Gold 200

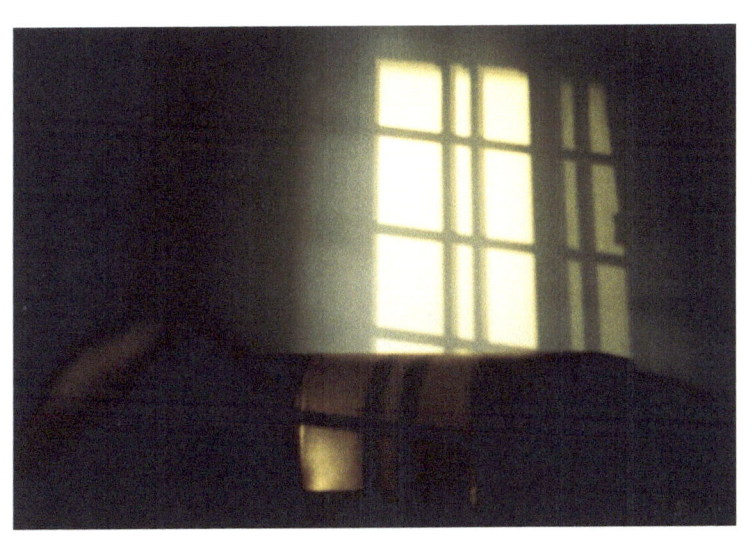

Canon AE-1 Program + Kodak Gold 200

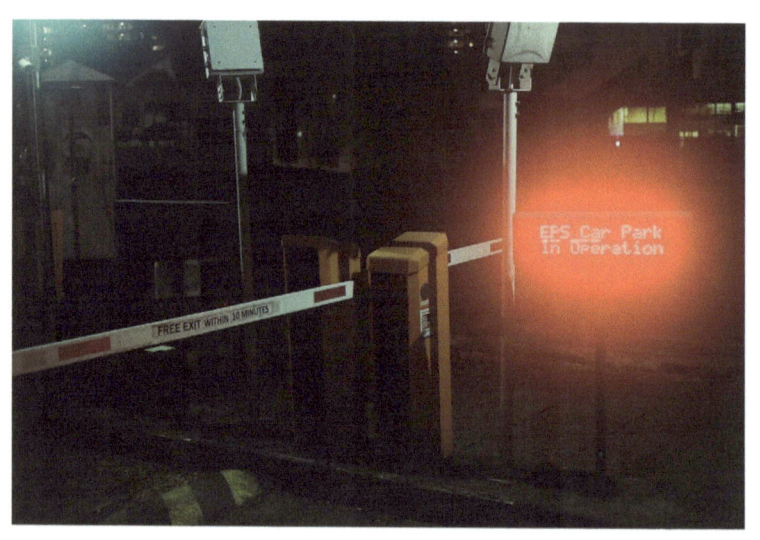

Canon AE-1 Program + Kodak Gold 200

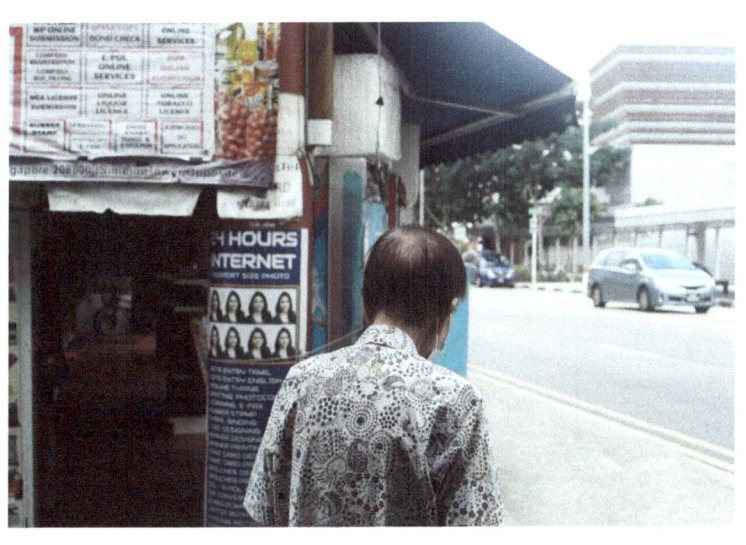

Canon AE-1 Program + Kodak Ultramax 400

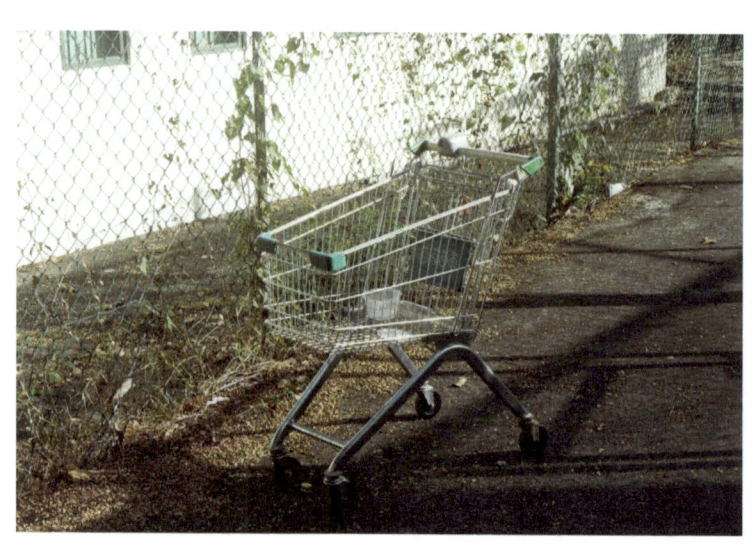

Canon AE-1 Program + Kodak Colorplus 200

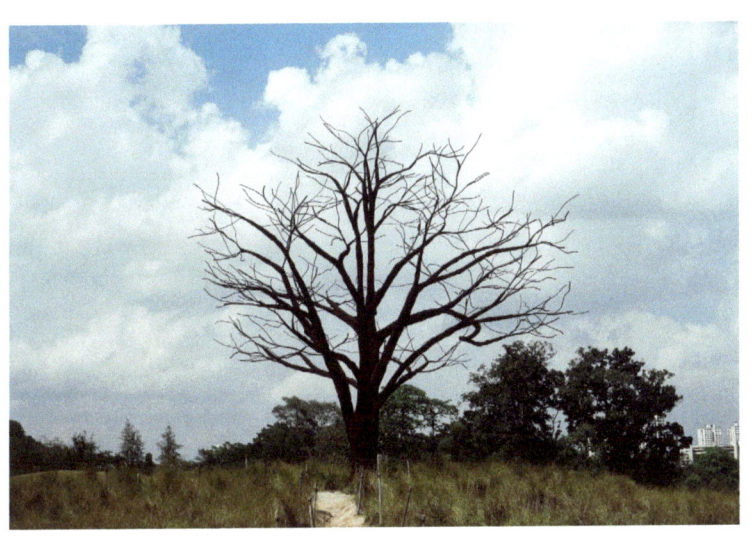

Canon AE-1 Program + Kodak Ultramax 400

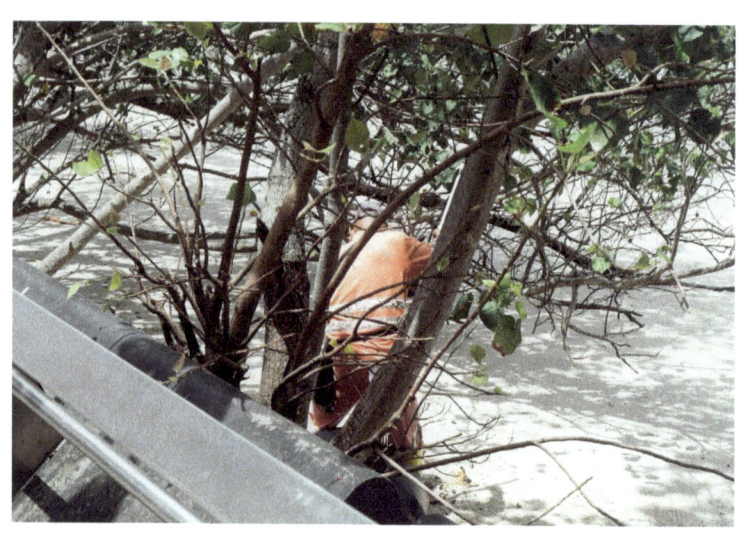

Canon AE-1 Program + Kodak Gold 200

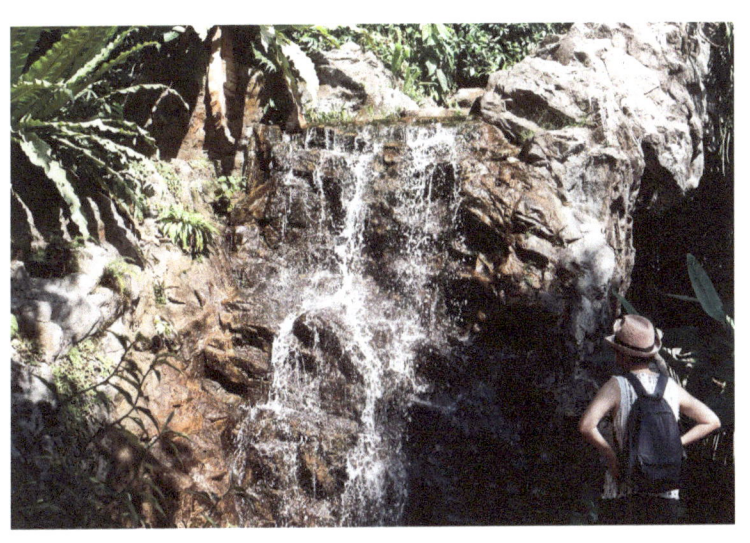

Canon AE-1 Program + Fuji Superia X-tra 400

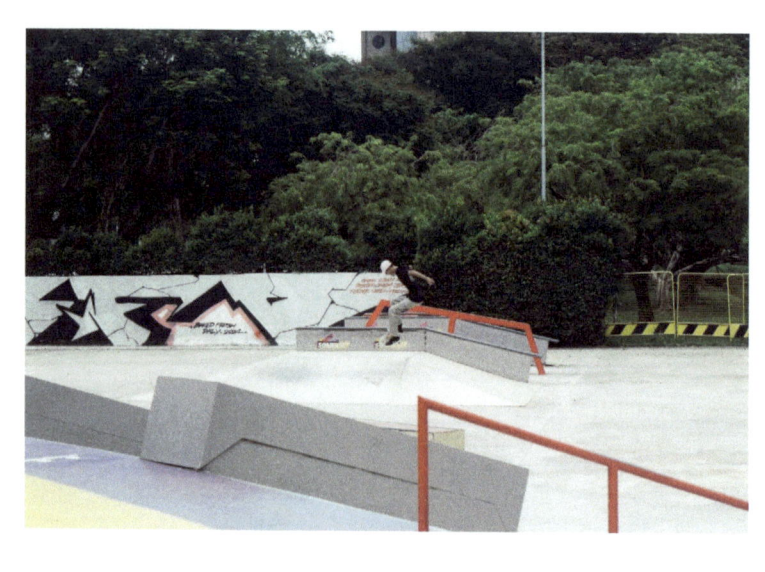

Canon AE-1 Program + Kodak Colorplus 200

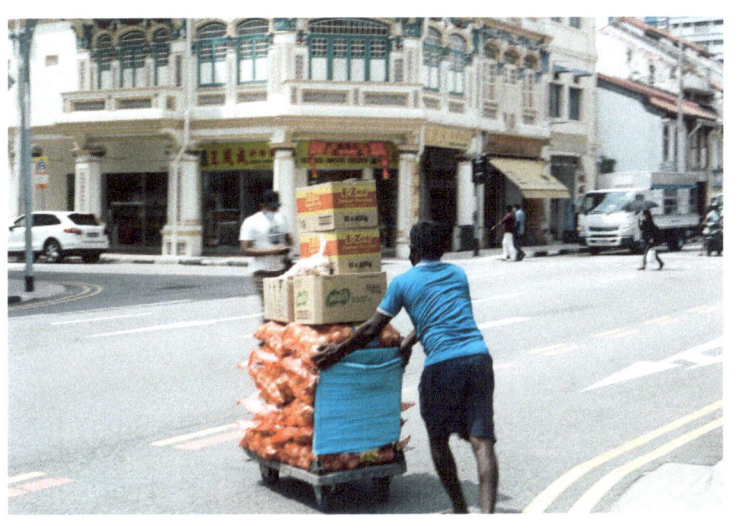

Canon AE-1 Program + Kodak Portra 400

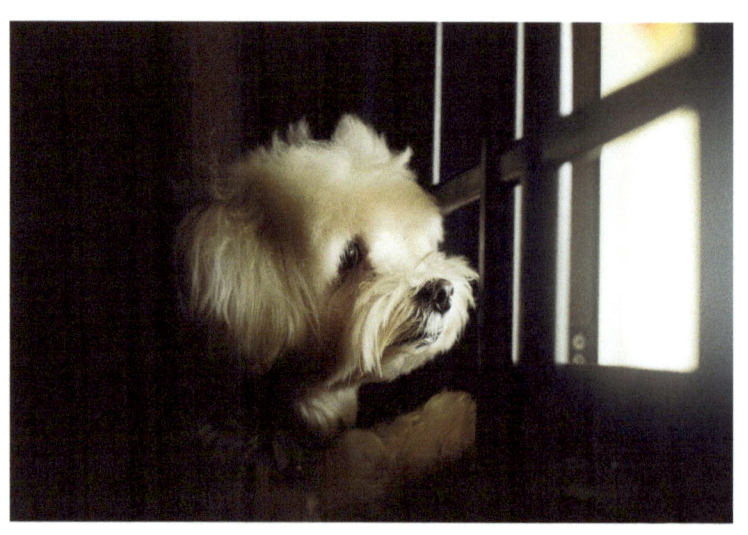

Canon AE-1 Program + Kodak Colorplus 200

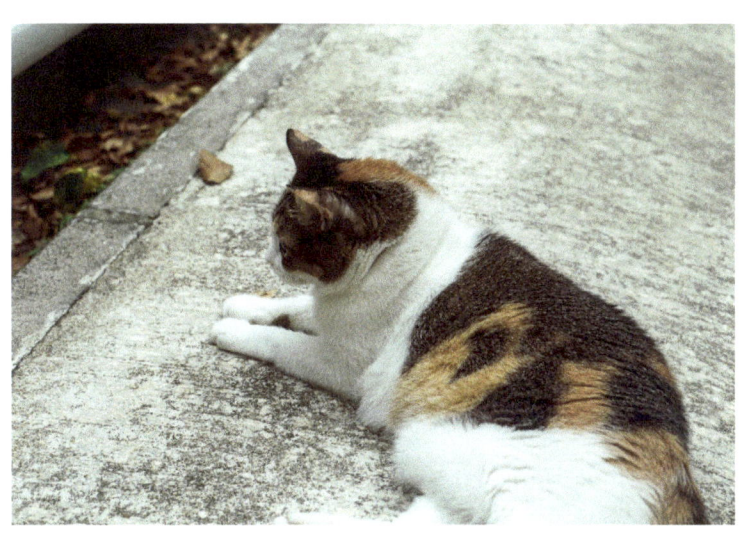

Canon AE-1 Program + Kodak Gold 200

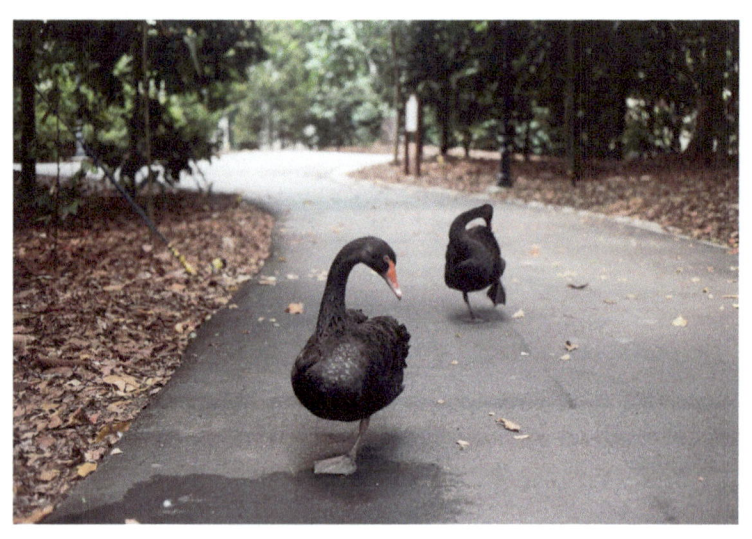

Canon AE-1 Program + Fuji Superia X-tra 400

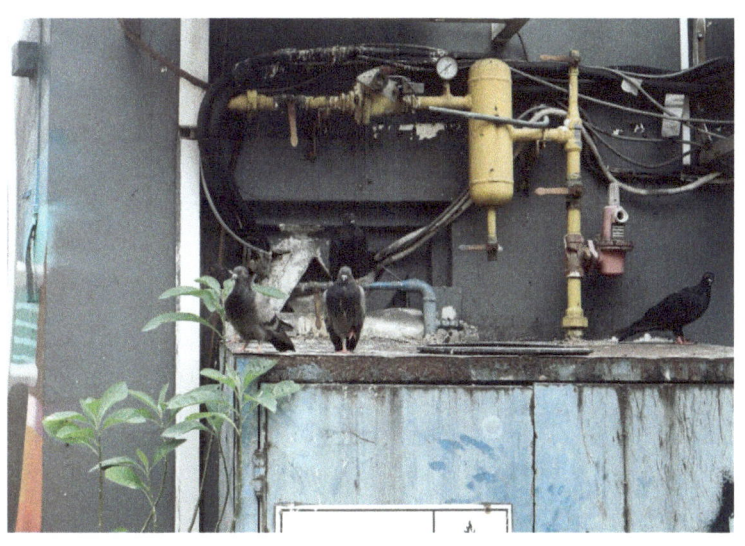

Canon AE-1 Program + Kodak Colorplus 200

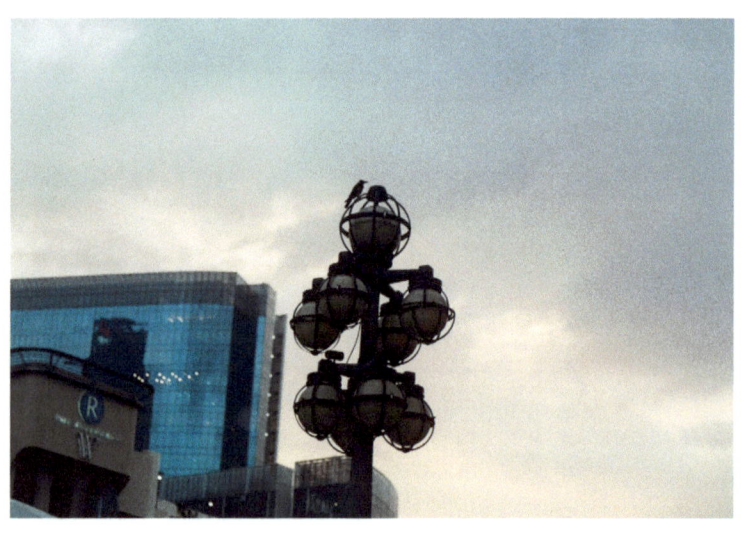

Canon AE-1 Program + Kodak Portra 400

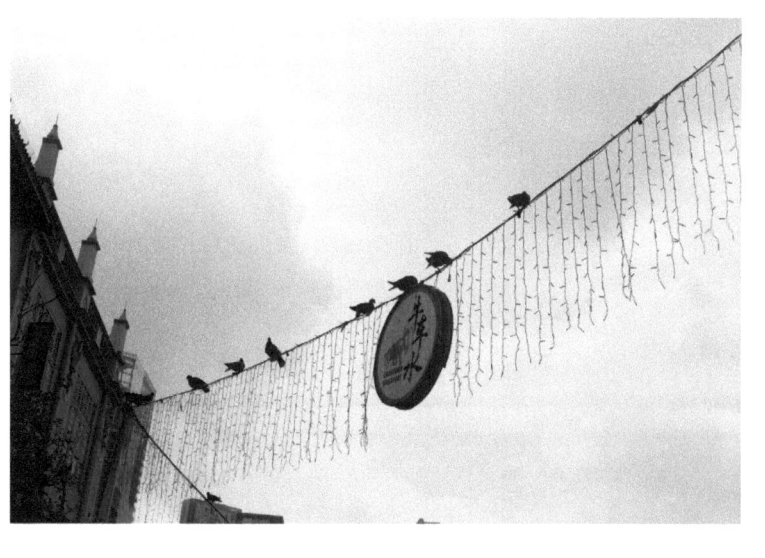

Canon AE-1 Program + Fuji Superia X-tra 400

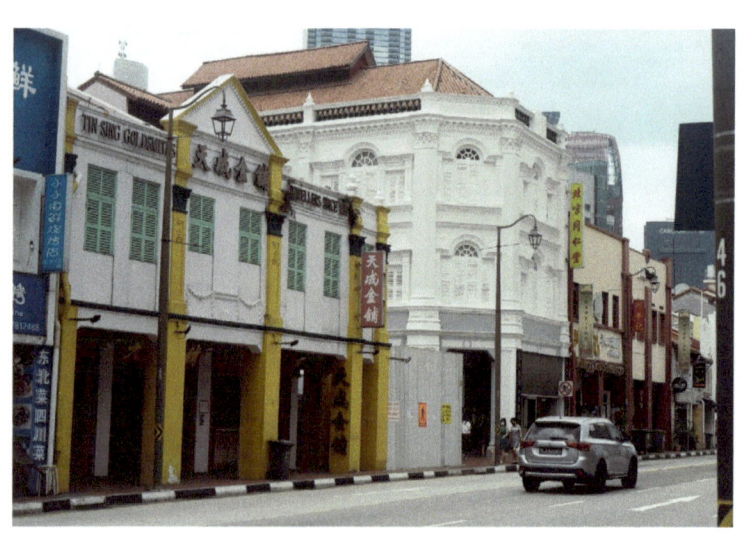

Canon AE-1 Program + Kodak Colorplus 200

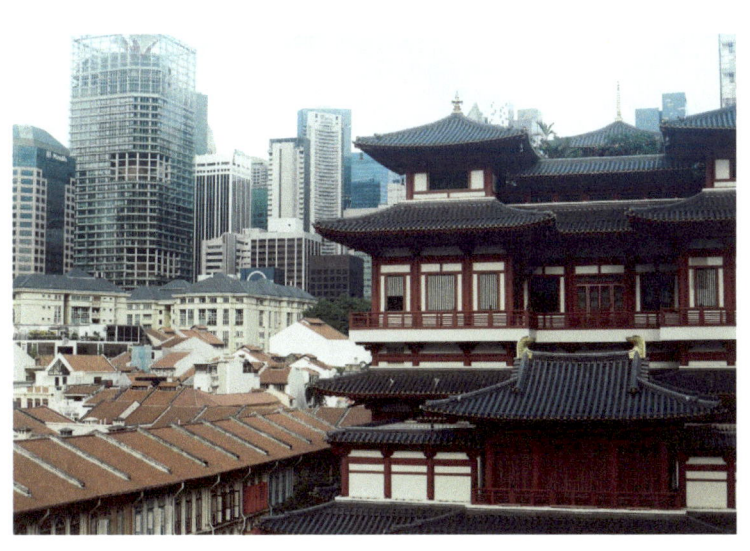

Canon AE-1 Program + Kodak ProImage 100

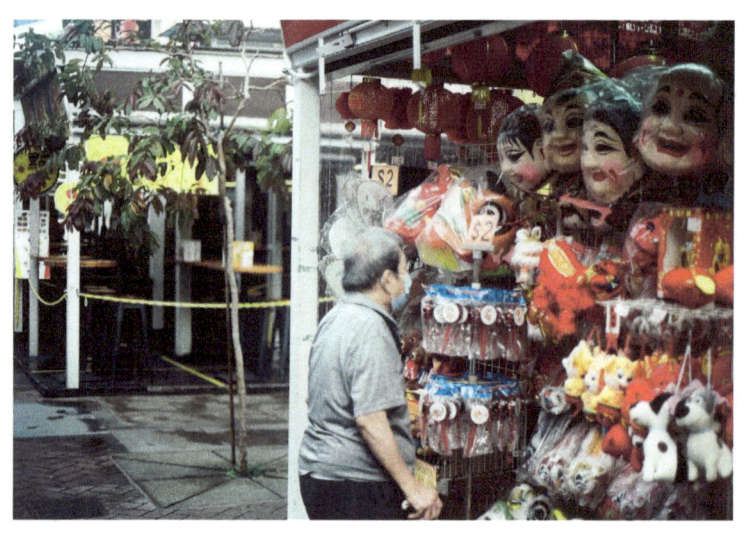

Canon AE-1 Program + Kodak ProImage 100

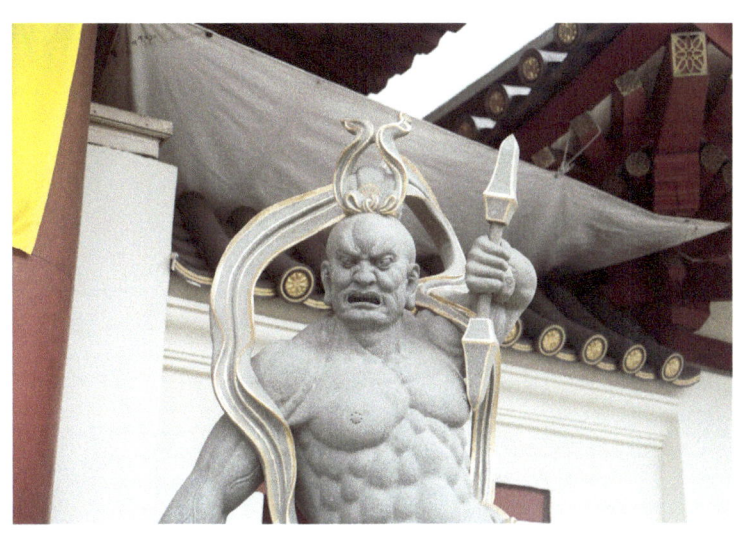

Canon AE-1 Program + Kodak Colorplus 200

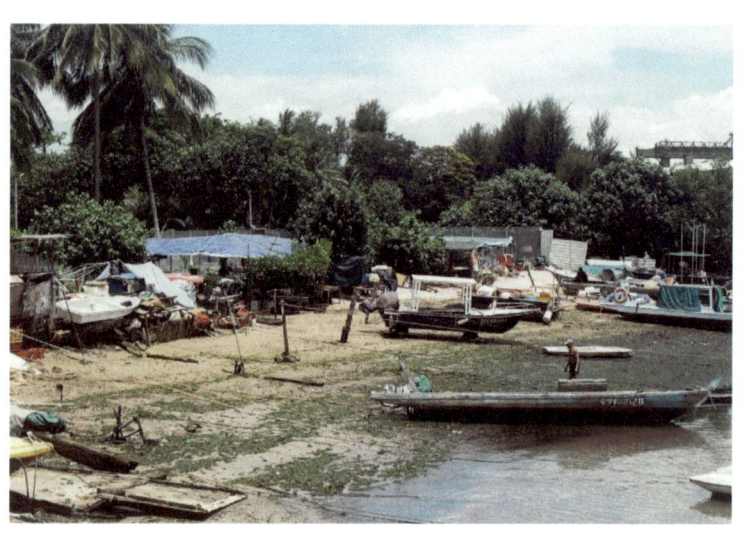

Canon AE-1 Program + Kodak ProImage 100

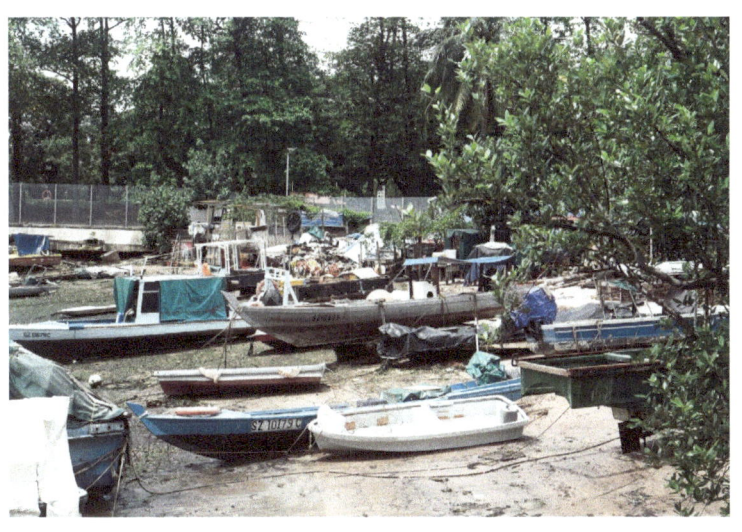

Canon AE-1 Program + Kodak ProImage 100

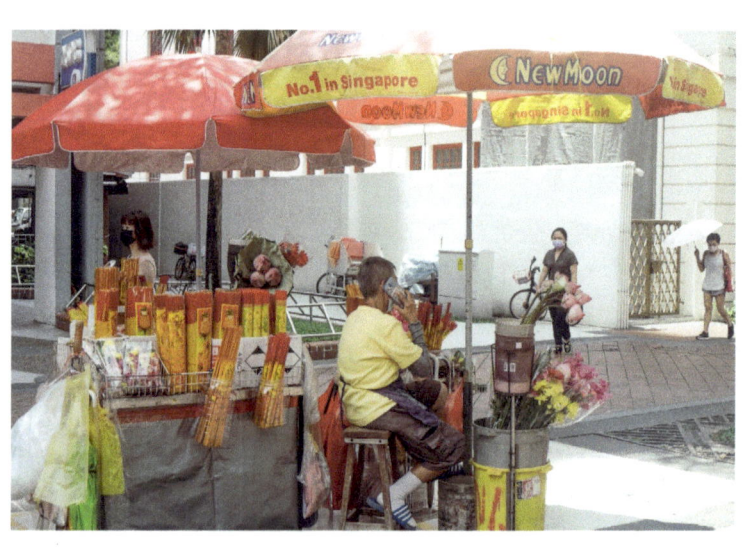

Canon AE-1 Program + Kodak Colorplus 200

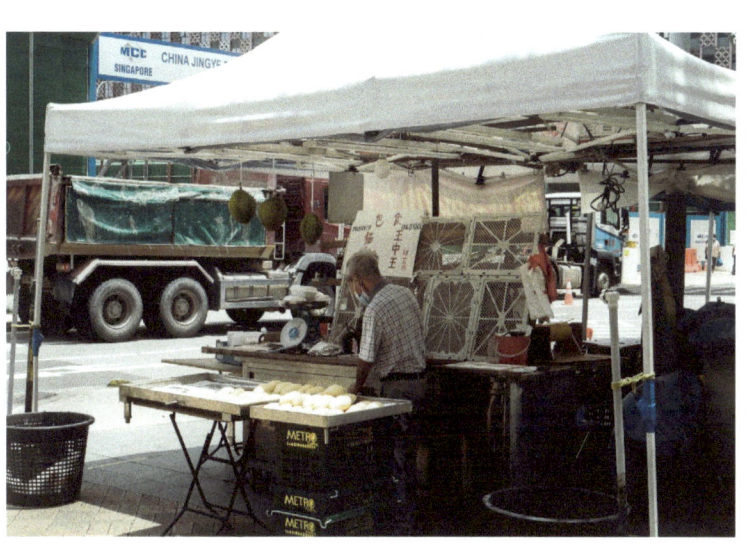

Canon AE-1 Program + Kodak Colorplus 200

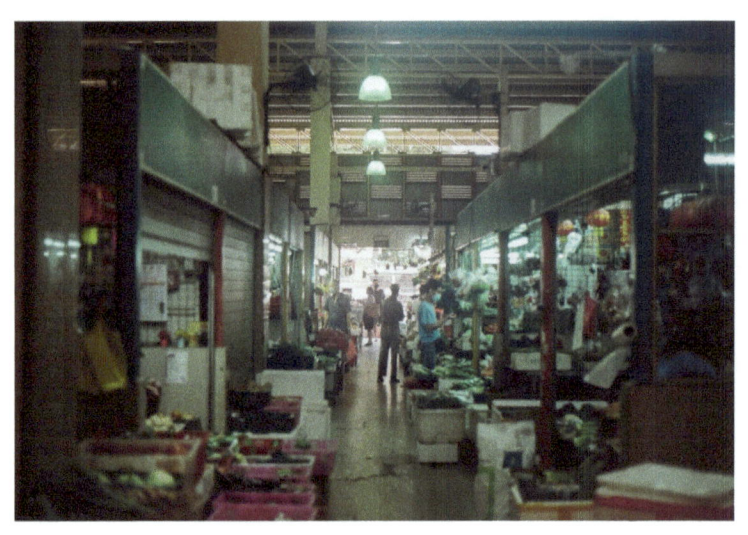

Canon AE-1 Program + Kodak ProImage 100

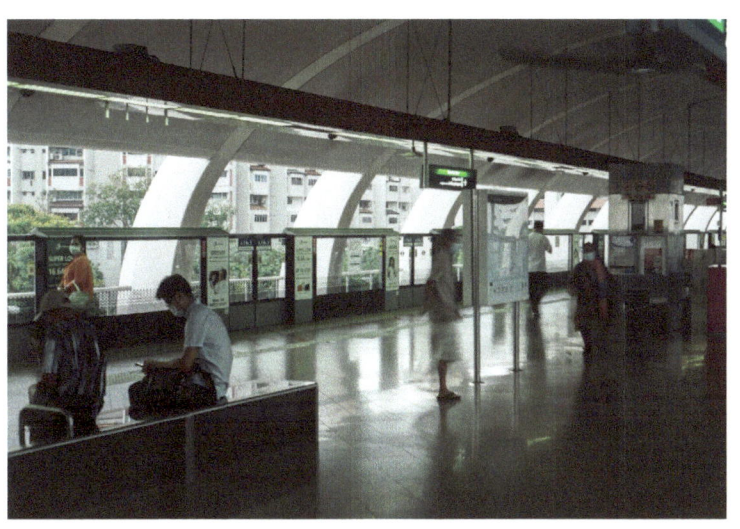

Canon AE-1 Program + Kodak ProImage 100

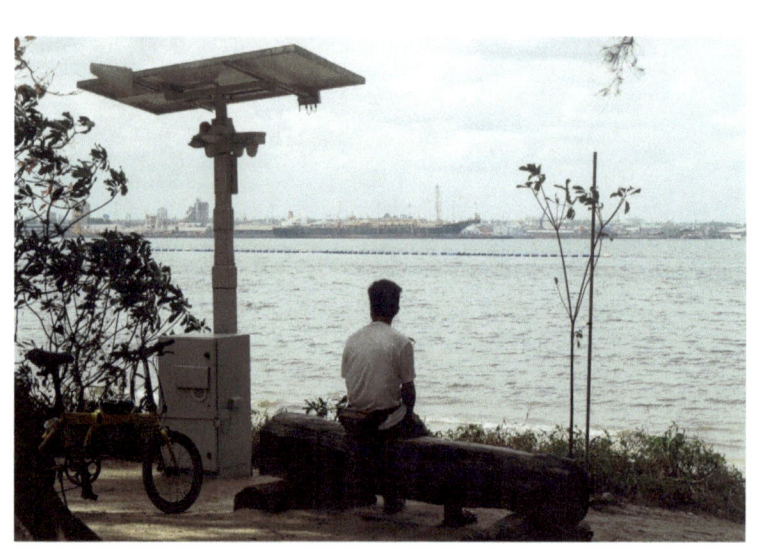

Canon AE-1 Program + Kodak Gold 200

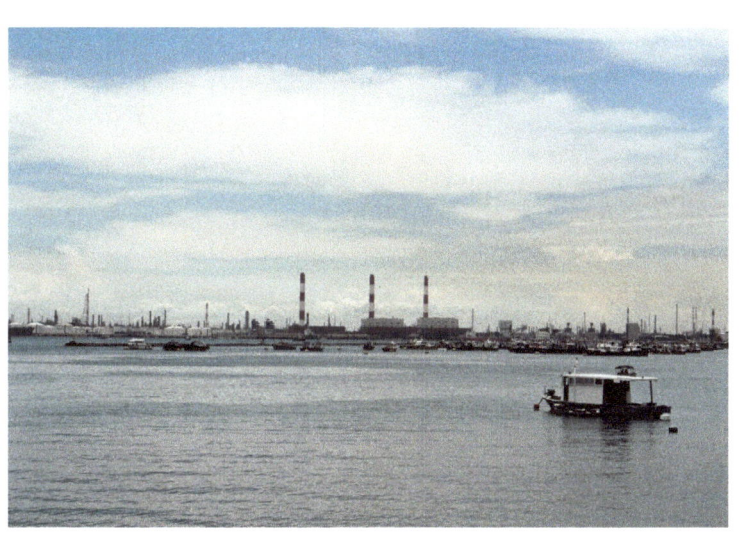

Canon AE-1 Program + Kodak ProImage 100

The title of this zine "The First Exposure" is a nod to the very first exposure of every roll of film and it also insinuates my first exposure to this whole new hobby (film photography).

This zine is created by me as a form of appreciation to the pictures I have taken throughout the course of my first 10 rolls of films. I personally think that by curating some of my favourite shots from the 10 rolls of film into a book is much more meaningful as compared to simply just uploading them on Instagram. I realised that by posting on Instagram, it sort of demoralises me especially when I don't get a certain amount of likes I expected to get. This is the toxicity of social media and I admit, I got sucked into it. On a personal level, this zine serves as a memento of my current obsession of film photography (which I have no idea if I am going to stop doing in the near future) and this also serves as a "hard copy" of my images apart from the negatives.

END

www.ingramcontent.com/pod-product-compliance
Lightning Source LLC
Chambersburg PA
CBHW040330220526
45473CB00009B/2631